Gardens

Gardens

Edited By Gary Takle
With Text By Emma Peacock

think

Think Publishing Australia
ABN 97 131 984 128
PO Box 448,
South Morang, Victoria 3752
Australia
Telephone: +61 3 9404 5579
info@thinkpublishing.com.au
www.thinkpublishing.com.au

© Think Publishing Australia, 2012

ISBN 978-0-9871356-8-1

Editor: Gary Takle
Writer: Emma Peacock
With Contributions by Corey Thomas

Graphic Design: Jonathan Takle and Tristan Wilson

Front and Back Cover Photography:
Lutsko Associates - SF Residence
Photography by Marion Brenner

Sponsored by Maison: A European Design

Andy Sturgeon Landscape & Garden Design Ltd. –
M&G Investments Chelsea 2012 Show Garden
Photograph provided by Andy Sturgeon

5

Contents

fontaine.

About

Aloha Pools essentially began in 1966, though it was only named as such a decade later, after founder Lindsay Fell passed the business on to his son Greg. What was once an all-encompassing landscaping practice then became focused exclusively on the design and construction of swimming pools – Greg's favourite feature of a garden. "At Aloha Pools we believe that a beautiful pool must begin on the design board and remain stunning twenty years on," he says.

The team at Aloha are equipped to undertake projects of any scale, from courtyard plunge pools to Olympic-sized commercial projects, roof-top spas to resort-style lagoons. Their specialty is in high-end domestic undertakings and difficult constructions in demanding locations.

Aloha Pools
3/35 Lakewood Boulevard
Carrum Downs, Victoria 3201, AUSTRALIA
T: +61 3 9775 0033
www.alohapools.com.au

This innovative concept by garden designer Paul Bangay contrasts the strikingly deep blue water of the pool with the warm sandy tones of the natural stone coping nearby. The depth of colour in the water is produced by the mid-blue ceramic tiles that line the pool surfaces.

Fontaine

A theme of European grandeur pervades the rear yard of this inner city house. The classical design of the swimming pool fits in perfectly with the environment created by the home's traditional architecture and is bolstered by a water feature and formal planting motif.

A number of stone design features contribute to the European styling of the space. Of particular note is the central water feature; a framed urn that fills the garden with the soothing sound of running water. In addition, the planting scheme is strategically arranged to subtly enhance the elegant, classical aesthetic of the garden and pool area.

Found alongside the dividing fence is an attractive flowerbed that conceals the neighbouring property with a screen of natural greenery, while simultaneously working in conjunction with the existing tennis court and foliage to emphasise the swimming pool and further integrate the outdoor entertaining area with the home.

The inclusion of both solar and gas heating ensures that the central swimming pool is accessible all year round, and not limited to a short summer season. Further, the in-floor cleaning system eliminates the need for manual vacuuming, while the automatic levelling device maintains the water at the optimum level.

The clever use of space in this design, such as holding close to the boundary and gently framing the garden areas, fulfilled the client's wishes in a unique and timeless way.

Photography by: George Kochukudiyil

Relying on the strong formal elements of a traditional European garden, it is nonetheless the originality and innovation behind this design that makes it such a success.

winston.

Aloha Pools
3/35 Lakewood Boulevard
Carrum Downs, Victoria 3201, AUSTRALIA
T: +61 3 9775 0033
www.alohapools.com.au

Carefully layered plants soften the harder aspects of the design, giving the garden depth and reducing the optical impact of such a long pool in a small yard.

Winston

The sweet, simple impact of this refreshing pool design belies its dual functionality. Serving as both a lap pool for exercise and a children's plunge pool, the crisp blue water adds a special visual flair to the outside environment.

The heritage nature of the house required a pool design that would cross boundaries, incorporating elements of both the modern functionality of the outdoor space and the traditional, formal elements of the home. In the resulting project, simplicity and balance enhance the pool and ensure it sits as a perfect counterweight to the garden.

The tile colour choice and elegant landscaping successfully integrated the new pool with the existing home. Constructed in reinforced concrete and finished in ceramic mosaic tiles, the combined pool space wraps around the garden with natural charm. The classic urn water feature adds an element of tranquillity to the garden, which is especially effective when the pool is not in use, yet it also strengthens the subtle classical theme that ties the outdoor environment to the house.

Finished with delicate tiles, the combination lap and play pool ripples around the alfresco dining area and continues throughout the garden. Fences have been cleverly concealed behind walls of foliage, resulting in a pool that achieves an organic quality and completes lavish outdoor space.

An informed choice of swimming pool equipment, including the in-floor cleaning system, the automatic sanitisers and high quality fixtures and fittings, resulted in minimal maintenance and maximum usage. The use of top quality products makes the area look elegant and takes nothing from the functionality of the space.

Photography by: Ben Wrigley

bayside.

About

Andrew Stark has been involved in horticulture all
his life, and has been designing gorgeous European-
inspired outdoor spaces for ten years.

"I like to create gardens for customers that are not only
a visual treat but ones in which they can get out and do
a little bit of gardening themselves, or walk through,
smell a fragrant flower or just sit and enjoy the space. I
like customers to enjoy their garden – that's one of my
philosophies, and it seems to work."

When designing his projects, Andrew considers 100%
of the house and how his garden will affect and reflect
its aesthetics and features. "The house will usually
dictate the style of the garden, and so does the lifestyle
of the client. Certainly, the house plays a major role
in the layout – where the windows and doors are, for
example, and the approach to the house."

Andrew Stark
PO Box 6
Mt. Eliza, Victoria 3930, AUSTRALIA
T: +61 419 597 494
www.astarkgardendesign.com.au

Large, ornate urns are dotted around the garden in symmetrical fashion, further highlighting the elegance of the design and providing visual links with the colour of the home.

Bayside

A statement of beauty and elegance is here defied in no uncertain terms. With manicured hedges and blossoming white roses abounding, the garden sits in wonderful assimilation with the architecture that acts as its picturesque backdrop.

A truly elegant design by Andrew Stark, this breathtaking garden inspires thoughts of 17th century royalty and eminence. Complementing the home's archetypal grand design, a wash of rich green foliage can be seen far off into the distance. Heavily manicured hedges and shrubs, along with perfectly trimmed lines of topiary spheres which sit beneath mature Canary Island Date Palms, bolster the grandeur of the design.

Centred in the yard is the impressive three-metre high 'Versailles' urn, creating the major site - line axis, linking the garden to the home. Floral embellishments also feature along the front of the home, in the form of gorgeous white 'Iceberg' roses.

The intricacies are what truly set this outdoor area apart, with selective shrubs featuring minimal floral elements, creating a point of difference in design, whilst providing a pleasant perfume as you walk by.

At the rear of the property, a similar theme is on show, with a more 'complimentary' selection of plants giving height to the design, and creating a superior sense of depth. A generously sized area of lawn is also present, catering for garden parties of the formal kind, as well as providing a place that children may play during the day.

Repetition and symmetry are overarching features of this outstanding project, boasting formality and distinction among beauty and elegance, revealing a place fit for the party of a king.

Along with its composition and layout, a difference in elevation helps to make the garden a centrepiece of the property, while the home sits gracefully behind. Imposing from the street, the splendour of this garden can only be admired from within its hedged boundaries.

Photography by: Andrew Stark

Low lying shrubbery defines the contrasting pathways of white quartz chips, leading guests through the immaculate garden and around the features it so astoundingly showcases.

My Father's
garden.

Andrew Stark
PO Box 6
Mt. Eliza, Victoria 3930, AUSTRALIA
T: +61 419 597 494
www.astarkgardendesign.com.au

Formic and inspired, this complex, structural garden pays tribute to classic design.

My Father's Garden

Striking a balance between spheres and squares, there's a lot to love about this elegant garden. Andrew Stark's trademark European classic style is on full display in this ornate design. The shape and layout of the garden is formic and precise, but a gentle planting scheme and classical sculptures give the environment a relaxed, inviting aspect.

Privacy and contemplative solitude pervade in this gracefully executed design. A lush, green wall of plants surrounds the entire space, balanced by layered hedges and leading inward to a central water feature and courtyard. The layout is an exercise in control, equally ornate and restrained. The garden is enclosed, yet provides ample breathing room.

The colour palette of the garden is limited, with white pebbles and sculptures balancing the rich and pervasive greens. Only the occasional brick border or bright yellow lemons interrupt the soothing, simple interaction of the largely dichromatic space.

Central to the design is a bronze fountain water feature, surrounded by an intricate parterre garden. A place for contemplation, this area then leads to a hardscaped patio, which in turn opens to another circular garden designed around an antique sundial. From this intimate space, pebble paths lead to smaller garden rooms, which feature life size imported Italian statuary. Tall boundary hedges allow for further privacy and solitude even in the context of the larger garden.

Crisp, subdued, and effortlessly stylish, the eye for detail and attention to form and balance that Andrew Stark's gardens embody is highlighted with clarity in this outdoor space. This series of exterior rooms, each connected to form one defining space, pays tribute to the strict control over nature and the attention to form and interplay that classical garden design demands.

Photography by: Andrew Stark and Tony Fawcett

A central water feature gives the garden a circular motif and provides a focal point for the design.

rosserdale.

Andrew Stark
PO Box 6
Mt. Eliza, Victoria 3930, AUSTRALIA
T: +61 419 597 494
www.astarkgardendesign.com.au

Hedging plays a feature role in the definition of the outdoor spaces. It is used both to frame garden beds and to create and separate the garden 'rooms'. Portugal Laurel (Prunus lusitanica) form a slightly higher trim than the extensively used English Box, making these zoned garden spaces feel unique and exotic.

Rosserdale

Building on a design he created to the front of the house, Andrew Stark implemented this formal but relaxed garden. It is both structured and geometric, softened with drifts and swaths of selected perennials to avoid a sense of compartmentalisation.

Large stone urns, handcrafted timber eaves and English Box (Buxus semipervirens) topiary spheres define a largely formal garden, but they also impart a kind of casual sensibility that afford the garden a softness and warmth.

The cased garden beds offer both a colourful and textural element to the garden, and the layering effect draws the eye up toward the featured elements of the planted spaces. Ornamental

Pears are under planted with white ball flowering Hydrangeas (Hydrangea macrophylla), whilst dwarf evergreen Magnolias (Magnolia grandiflora 'Teddy Bear') punctuate each garden corner.

Perennial beds are mass planted with white flowering Rugosa Roses (Rosa rugosa alba), white flowering Mexican Sage (Salvia 'Velour White'), Spurge (Euphorbia 'Craigieburn' & E. 'Silver Swan'), fine leaf Oyster Plant (Acanthus spinulosus), Society Garlic (Tulbargia violacea alba) and Winter Rose (Helleborus x hybridus). Lambs Ears (Stachys lanata 'Big Ears') form a soft carpet through the beds.

The entertaining areas which run along the rear of the house enjoy a picturesque outlook over

the lovely garden. This space is paved by Anston 600 x 600 mm Bondi pavers, and these continue downwards, covering the steps. Hand painted white timber furniture matches accessories placed throughout the garden.

An exercise in symmetry, proportions and simplicity, this attractive landscape – filled with lush green foliage throughout the year with seasonal splashes of soft whites - is the perfect complement to the house and lifestyle of the owners. Offering ample space to entertain that overlooks the beautifully proportioned garden, this is an ideal outdoor space that is reserved and classical but equally warm and accessible.

The garden's boundaries are outlined by Ornamentaol Pears (Pyrus calleryana 'Cleveland Select'), that provide screening and continue the theme of softness with their snowy white blooms. The privacy suggested by these screens is further emphasized in the hedging that divides the garden.

Photography by: Andrew Stark

M&G Investments
Chelsea 2012 Show
garden.

About

Andy Sturgeon is one of the UK's leading garden designers, offering striking, contemporary designs that rely on natural materials and innovative planting. Having won six gold medals at the prestigious Chelsea Flower Show, including Best in Show in 2010, he regularly appears on TV and writes for numerous national newspapers and magazines.

Andy's practice creates bold, architectural and timeless landscapes, both within the UK and abroad, drawing on his wealth of experience to transform small spaces into inspirational outdoor rooms.

Andy Sturgeon Landscape & Garden Design Ltd.
20 Clermont Road
Brighton BN1 6SG, UNITED KINGDOM
T: +44 1 273 553 336
www.andysturgeon.com

Landscape Contractor:
Creative Landscape Co
T: +44 1 189 341500
www.creative-landscape.co.uk

The solidity of classical design and the energy of contemporary principles give this garden a unique and arresting strength.

M&G Investments Chelsea 2012 Show Garden

Built around the values of the M&G brand, this garden by Andy Sturgeon embodies three central notions: conviction, energy and originality. Elegantly articulated, sophisticated, and timeless, this garden lays its roots in traditional garden design, but grows from it with unique flair to ensure relevance and appeal.

The basic layout of the garden is linear and formal, with straight paths, steps and walls extending from a large, rectangular pond. This arrangement reflects the first of the garden's themes: conviction. Solid and dependable, it is the permanence and safety imparted by both the classical layout and the high walls that represents the integrity of the design.

The 'energy wave' sculpture that weaves through the garden is free and unconstrained, in direct contrast to the formal walls. This copper sculpture is a dramatic focal point, flexible and fluid, that works its way around the paths, paved area, and pool, balancing and contrasting with the traditional design elements without challenging or disrupting their visual strength.

Originality is reflected in the details of the garden. A long bench cuts through an aperture in the wall, appearing to float without obvious support. The three stone-clad walls are detailed with drilled holes, revealing a copper lining that links it to the welded 'energy wave' sculpture. Even the stone paths and paving, while smooth and elegant on top, are subtly contrasting, having rough-hewn and uneven edges.

Lively, informal and woodlands-style planting is given structure and form, with clipped domes of Ilex crenata and massed spikes of Equisetum. The rounded leaves of the Cercidiphyllum trees echo the circular motif, while the coppery pink tinge of the new foliage in spring will further harmonise with the sculpture. The plantings, though clearly manicured, serve to soften the built elements with their organic warmth.

Inspired by the traditional craftsmanship and ornate design of the Arts and Crafts movement, the structure and form of this garden give it stability. The space is effortlessly graceful and subtly modern.

Plants:

Katsura - Cercidiphyllum japonicum
Garden Angelica - Angelica archangelica
Cow Parsley - Anthriscus sylvestris
Meadow Rue - Thalictrum 'Black Stockings'

Unlike many show gardens, this design could be comfortably adapted as a true garden, perhaps attached to an equally architectural and dynamic home.

Ferntree **gully.**

About

Highly respected in the landscaping industry for his humble approach and award winning projects, Matt Seymour, co-director of Apex Landscapes, continuously raises the bar of outdoor design through his high attention to detail, customisation and strong workmanship.

Matt established Apex Landscapes in 2005 as a sole trader. Working in conjunction with his esteemed colleague Steve Blencowe, they each mentored one another through their respective new business challenges. Subsequently, it was a natural progression for them to develop into business partners, with Steve joining Matt as co-owner of Apex Landscapes Pty Ltd in 2006.

Apex Landscapes
PO BOX 299
Chelsea, Victoria 3196, AUSTRALIA
T: +61 3 9772 8617
www.apexlandscapes.com.au

Upon entering the garden, guests are greeted with an outlook of relaxation and enjoyment, a place that could effortlessly facilitate some of the most peaceful and pleasant moments you could imagine having in your own home.

Ferntree Gully

An impeccable outdoor entertainment area is showcased in a stunning display of resort-style living. Designed by Apex Landscapes, it features three separate spaces that each fulfil a specific purpose. The main entertainment section is raised, while zones for the kids sit just below and to the rear of the gorgeous sunken spa to allow them to enjoy the sun. Due to steep grades in the land, each outdoor area was designed in exacting detail, with innovation at the forefront of the initiative.

A fully appointed alfresco kitchen is the hero of this articulate design, featuring a double bar fridge, four burner barbecue and sink, as well as a stainless steel range-hood. With down lighting installed in each of the pavilions, cooking, dining and entertaining is effortless at any time of the day or night. The inclusion of a large Hamii Bamboo creates a notable feature to one end of the deck, its stripped stems acting as a focal point, while low profile outdoor sofas allow for maximum comfort.

Following the Cycads that flank the edge of the raised alfresco kitchen area, guests are led onto the first section of lawn, where the kids are able to play freely while the adults watch on from the second pavilion a little further along. A padded bench seat also sits here, at the head of a large and inviting spa.

Located just behind this pavilion is another grassed area, raised higher again, which is slightly enclosed by the overhanging trees and lush foliage, creating a place to escape the monotony of everyday life.

With ample space to enjoy and comfort to flaunt, entertaining in this garden is sure to be special.

Photography by: Tim Turner

On the lower level of the outdoor area, bluestone paving lines the floor, creating a place on which to dine in the open air. Surrounded by Agaves, Hosta, Kentia Palms and even more Cycads, a natural balance is achieved to offset the 'constructed' elements of the environment.

Camero

courtyard.

About

Ketti Kupper is a multi-disciplinary artist and designer
on HGTV with published work awarded by gallery
directors and art critics. She's made gardens for
celebrities and paintings for American Express and
Silver Burdette amongst others.

Known for her architectural, art-infused landscapes,
mixed media paintings, portraits, poetry and bas
relief sculptures, Ketti's distinctive mix of modern
and old world sensibilities stand alone. Projects range
from large scale public art landscapes to intimate
healing gardens and personal motivation fine art and
decorative art.

Ketti Kupper
Conscious Living Landscapes
Los Angeles, California, United States of America
T: +1 323 868 3558
www.consciouslivinglandscapes.com

This small, intimate garden demanded material expression that would hold up under scrutiny. Images and messages that inspire and describe the artist decorate the space.

Camero Courtyard

On the eastern-most fringe of the West Side of Los Angeles in a neighbourhood shaped by an eclectic range of nationalities and aesthetics sits this "East Hollywood" bungalow, home to artist Ketti Kupper. The range of stylistic reference points, the views of downtown Los Angeles and the artist's personal style have informed the construction of a chic, individual and beautiful garden space.

The courtyard makeover annexes more living spaces from the front of the property, establishing a space for peace and tranquility. Three of the artist's works feature a teal/grey colour scheme analogous to the palette of the house, and these vinyl canvas prints are calming, unique visual features that create a serene but determined ambience in the space.

'Five Graces' is theatrical, sitting against a backdrop of the twinkling hillside lights at night and the patina of the steel during the daylight. 'Meet Yourself There' is a vertical figure, reminding anyone that exits the sanctuary of the courtyard that we always carry the opportunity to take our own true identity into the world outside.

To the west, 'Bearings' is a projection of thought-provoking explorations. Developed with reference to Hokusai's 'The Great Wave', the painting communicates the importance of finding one's bearings before venturing into the day to make life-choices.

The planting scheme cues extend from existing Japanese conifers along the driveway, supplying a subtle Eastern theme that extends to the hard elements. The benches in the garden are lower than the norm, yet another subtle Japanese influence. The underside of the benches are lined with rope LED lighting, giving the garden a magical feeling at night.

The subtle but diverse material choices throughout this garden give it depth and a sense of poise and contemplation. Images and messages that inspire reflection, introspection and observation are placed thoughtfully throughout the garden, imbuing the space with personality.

Photography by: Ashley Elizabeth Ford and Ketti Kupper

The poetic encounters and metal plaques throughout the garden establish a thematic notion of unanswered questions – there is the sense in this deep and encapsulating garden that there is more space to explore, and a hidden mystery at every turn. A pond just outside the office window connects the tranquil sound and calm energy of running water to the owner's office.

Caulfield

north.

About

COS Design, formerly Creative Outdoor Solutions, have been designing and constructing award winning landscapes since it was founded in 2000 by managing director, Steve Taylor. Working in conjunction with leading architects, builders and directly with the client, Steve Taylor and the team offer a multi-award winning service that starts at the first point of contact and is approached at every level with the utmost professionalism, innovation, creativity and construction detail.

COS Design offer a complete professional landscape service from design through to construction and follow up maintenance to suit individual site needs.

COS Design
392 Burke Road
Camberwell, Victoria 3124, AUSTRALIA
T: +61 3 9889 3328
www.creativeoutdoorsolutions.com.au

The expansive pool is a glittering feature. Soothing green bisazza mosaic bands and a raised wall highlights the slender weaver bamboo, creating a stunning backdrop that lends atmosphere to the entire space and offers privacy from neighbouring properties.

Caulfield North

Modern, minimal undertones of Eastern design weave elegantly through this cleanly designed contemporary outdoor space. Bold lines, floating benches, a restrained palette and a balanced conceptualization of the space have resulted in a timeless and effortless garden.

The owners of this attractive modern home were seeking a sleek, clean timeless outdoor space that would allow for relaxed, informal al fresco entertaining. The space had to be visually striking, feature a large family pool and sit amongst a lush yet minimal plant palette.

The effortless functional layout of the space ensures that it can be used on a daily basis by every member of the family, but the balanced, well conceptualized space ensures it opens up easily for larger numbers when required.

The expansive pool is a glittering feature. Soothing green bisazza mosaic bands and a raised wall highlights the slender weaver bamboo, creating a stunning backdrop that lends atmosphere to the entire space and offers privacy from neighbouring properties. The outdoor shower highlight wall and the floating bench seat to the rear perfectly balances the space.

The al fresco area sits beneath an Aludean laser cut screen, creating a highlight that provides valuable light into the space. The floating teppanyaki barbecue is a functional and formal aesthetic highlight that stylishly enhances the space.

The planting scheme is inviting and bold, but minimal. The Japanese maple adds a living architectural sculpture that references the subtle Asiatic theme of the space. Cliveas fill the lower level of the design with lush vibrant floral displays, and the black Cordyline softens the crisp white walls that define the area.

Every moment in this garden is considered. A floating plinth highlights the front entry, the perfect invitation into the home. It references the importance of water to the design, as it gently trickles down the sides into a lower fishpond. This sophisticated, simple and elegant garden space is of the finest quality, the perfect context for the outdoor life of the family.

Every moment in this garden is considered. A floating plinth highlights the front entry, the perfect invitation into the home.

Garrell

street.

COS Design
392 Burke Road
Camberwell, Victoria 3124, AUSTRALIA
T: +61 3 9889 3328
www.creativeoutdoorsolutions.com.au

The subtle sound of flowing water
creates a special ambience. Trekking
a path down the feature wall and over
the edge of the spa, this gentle water
feature encloses the space.

Garrell Street

Exceeding the highest expectations of the proud owner, this beautiful garden is a spectacular complement to the house it surrounds, adding not only new aesthetic depth to the client's home but an accompaniment to their lifestyle as well.

The front yard is framed by a unique architectural front fence and entry portico. The shadow-lined Anston blade wall doubles as a bench seat within the property, providing a quiet space for relaxation and overlooking bands of Black Mondo as well as the lush buffalo lawn.

A Maple with under-planted Gardenias breaks up the mass of hard surfaces that define the space, softening the architectural forms of the garden. The Cliveas are implemented to the same end

and create a bright visual highlight beneath the matching timber blades. The large format Anston pavers are broken up with the recurring thematic planting of black mondo strips. The structural form of an Aloe tree in a raised planter box defines the entryway and links the front space to a similar feature in the rear garden.

A striking pool and spa combination is the focal point of the backyard. Architecturally, the beautiful, fluid elements that comprise the pool and spa are crafted to complement the design of the home; simultaneously sharp and inviting, bold and soft, these have been perfectly conceived to connect naturally to the house. A poolside lounge area abuts the space, sheltered by the extended eaves of the home – perfect for relaxing.

The subtle sound of flowing water creates a special ambience. Trekking a path down the feature wall and over the edge of the spa, this gentle water feature encloses the space. The Aloe tree – analogous to the one at the front of the home – brings liveliness to the space. Under-planted by Scencio Chalk Sticks to soften the sculptural tree, this subtle link ties the design together.

Extending directly from the home's living space is an alfresco dining area, where a chunky cedar arbor hovers overhead, adding warmth to the dining area, which flows onto the tennis court and children's play space. An angled, cantilevered barbecue and built in floating bench seat adds functionality and architectural flair to the garden.

Photography by: Tim Turner

A striking pool and spa combination is the focal point of the backyard. Architecturally, the beautiful, fluid elements that comprise the pool and spa are crafted to complement the design of the home

Radnor St.

camberwell.

COS Design
392 Burke Road
Camberwell, Victoria 3124, AUSTRALIA
T: +61 3 9889 3328
www.creativeoutdoorsolutions.com.au

A beautiful lighting scheme brings depth to the garden at night, and the considered planting scheme and beautiful hardscaped spaces ensure it is inviting at any time of day.

Radnor St Camberwell

The landscaped spaces that surround this inner-city home are simple and sophisticated. As a dominant feature of the streetscape and a defining frame for the home it adorns, the site required an innovative and striking design. Steve Taylor of COS Design has composed a stunning and highly functional garden that not only softens the unique architecture of the new build home, but complements the modern interior, flows naturally over pre-set levels and reconciles the slight architectural conflict between the home and the poolside pavilion.

The front garden space features a large return driveway softened by flanking lush lawns and matched plantings. To the street boundary, a row of Agave varieties stretch out behind Ornamental Pears under planted with Heuchera Purple Palace for colour and contrasting texture. Along the front terrace, a row of Cycads under planted by Black

Mondo provide contrast to the weeping Japanese Maple along the side of the entry. Teddy Bear Magnolias line the side fences and complete the planting theme.

The tranquil inner courtyard created by the pool zone is the hero of the rear landscape. Sitting between the residence and the rear pavilion, this space is visible from every main entertaining space in the home, and it forms an enticing feature of the interior and the rear space.

To the rear of the spa lies a Spotted Gum deck, offering owners and guests a spot to relax by the pool and an additional architectural element that softens the transition between house and pavilion. A cantilevered bench seat is a fun and functional addition to this space, and a raised cobble plinth is another visual feature, bearing a lump fire bowl framed by a single Senkaki Maple to the rear.

The overall planting theme of the rear garden is extensive and thoughtful. Slender Weaver Bamboo was employed as a living architectural feature, providing privacy from the street. A modern splash comes in the form of staggered bands of Black Mondo that jut into the lush, tall fescue lawn, while alternating beds of Scencio Chalk Sticks and Bamboo frame the space, bringing the home and poolside pavilion together.

This landscaped space is dazzling and exciting – the only conceivable complement to a beautiful architectural home. A beautiful lighting scheme brings depth to the garden at night, and the considered planting scheme and beautiful hardscaped spaces ensure it is inviting at any time of day.

Photography by: Tim Turner

The tranquil inner courtyard created by the pool zone is the hero of the rear landscape. Sitting between the residence and the rear pavilion, this space is visible from every main entertaining space in the home, and it forms an enticing feature of both the interior and the rear space.

Mid-Century
revival.

About

Dane Spencer Landscape Architecture, located in Sarasota, Florida focuses on environmentally compatible exterior designs that are visually interesting and timeless. By using a plant palette of mostly native vegetation, Dane is able to create landscapes that are low maintenance, require less water resources and fit within the natural environment while providing habitat for native wildlife.

Considering water the most precious resource, Dane Spencer incorporates rainwater storage into his designs. The beauty of this approach is that the cisterns are integrated into the structure of the design, and are hidden, achieving a high aesthetic while reducing the water needs of the garden.

Dane Spencer Landscape Architecture
530 South Orange Avenue
Sarasota, Florida 34236, UNITED STATES OF AMERICA
T: +1 941 587 6512
www.danespencer-landscapearchitect.com

Unity in theme and construction complete
this tranquil outdoor environment. Water
weaves through the balanced design,
softening the strong lines and producing
a private oasis theme within the space.

Photo by Greg Wilson

Mid-Century Revival

Mid-century modern design meets the privacy and isolation of a quiet backyard retreat in this simply expressed outdoor space. The lines of the garden are clean, direct, and elegant, complementing the overall geometric design that forms the space. Plants soften the straight, hard edges of the home and the garden, blending the spaces and complementing the architecture.

Water has a strong thematic presence in the garden. The swimming pool is integral to the space, and waterfalls and rusted rain basins complete the integration while providing fish and plant habitat. The ambient trickle of running water enhances the private, isolated atmosphere of the space.

A large rainwater cistern captures and redistributes collected rainwater. The plant scheme is predominately native, with a mix of sub-tropicals providing visual diversity and a low maintenance habitat for wildlife. This subtle emphasis on the planted spaces draws focus to the natural element of the garden.

A shell and concrete pool and patio deck unifies the ground plane throughout the garden. Crushed shell is used in lower foot traffic areas to provide textural contrast while harmonizing with the integral shell concrete. Subtle structural changes to the interior of the home and an extended roof overhang has integrated the outdoor and indoor, and the textural flow is natural, with both spaces benefitting from the association.

Intimate, private and soothing without being crowded or overly designed, there is a simplicity to this design that gives it an edge. Sitting naturally against and integrating with the beautiful modern house and incorporating elements of 'green' sustainable sensibility, this garden will stand the test of time.

Plants:
Simpson Stopper - *Myrcianthes fragrans*
Flatwood Plum - *Prunus umbellata*
Pitch Apple - *Clusia rosea*
Seagrape – *Coccoloba uvifera*
Coontie – *Zamia floridana*
Blanket Flower – *Gaillardia pulchella*

Photography by: Giovani Lunardi Photography, with additional images by Greg Wilson (where noted)

This project is a collaboration between Dane Spencer Landscape Architecture and Greg Hall Architects, PA, and has recieved the 2012 Florida Gulf Coast AIA Award of Excellence, and the 2010 First Annual James Rose Award, Suburbia Transformed.

Nokomis

waterfront.

Dane Spencer Landscape Architecture
530 South Orange Avenue
Sarasota, Florida 34236, UNITED STATES OF AMERICA
T: +1 941 587 6512
www.danespencer-landscapearchitect.com

The waterside location adds the flair of
a private resort to this enticing design.

Nokomis Waterfront

Finding a beautiful middle ground between natural beach planting and tropical oasis has given this modern Mediterranean inspired home a colourful boost. Capturing the best of both worlds, the cheerful aesthetic is inviting and fresh, balancing the drought resistant naturalism of the "Old Florida" aesthetic with a more flamboyant planting scheme.

A diverse range of colours and textures gives this garden depth and a very deeply considered planting scheme ensures that the space is low maintenance and requires minimal water. The style is decidedly festive, organized and tropical, but has a relaxed beachside ambience that balances the harder elements. This is a place ideal for hanging out with a Margarita: there is nothing demanding or formal about this landscape.

The curvilinear retaining walls create the necessary scale for the success of the project. Lush plantings soften the hardscape, and the walls flow away from the house, directing views toward the water. Plants have been carefully implemented to provide unique atmospheres whether one is viewing the garden from the pool deck or from the ground.

Crushed shells are used to mimic the natural beach on the path behind the existing seawall. Surrounded by beach plantings, this natural space helps draw in native birds and wildlife.

Fun and inviting, but environment conscious and site appropriate, compromise between the garden designer and the client has resulted in the perfect garden to complement the home and location.

Salt tolerant, drought resistant plants, both native and introduced, require little water or maintenance and provide a range of textures in the inviting outdoor space.

Plants:
Silver Oxeye Daisy – *Borrichia aborescens*
Texas Sage – *Leucophyllum frutescens*
Sea Purslane – *Susuvium portuclacastrum*
Cast Iron Plant – *Aspidistra elatior*
Mammy Croton – *Codiaeum variegatum*
Hildebrandtii Cycad – *Encephalartos hildebrandtii*

Photography by: Giovani Lunardi Photography

Vibrant and inviting, this relaxed beachside garden strikes a compromise between modern and traditional, blending native and exotic plant life to match the home and lifestyle of the owners.

Firenze

project.

About

Domain Pools and Landscapes are a passionate company that have grown from one of Melbourne's leading and most awarded landscape builders into a company that provides clients with a full range of pool, landscape, water storage and combination design-construction services. They are at the forefront of the industry, working with many of Melbourne's leading architects and builders.

The company works closely with the client, listening to preferences, exploring innovative design options and coordinating construction. They gain an impression of your lifestyle and deliver a project that is beautiful, functional and liveable.

Tony McLeod, Managing Director

Domain Pools & Landscapes
PO Box 7191
Beaumaris, Victoria 3193, AUSTRALIA
T: +61 3 9585 1432
www.domainpoolsandlandscapes.com.au

Modern and geometric, this sleek pool and spa combination complements the bold lines of the architectural home it accompanies.

Firenze Project

Sitting beneath the imposing form of a handsome contemporary home, this sophisticated pool and spa design relies on simple shapes, solid lines and a strong material presence to balance the structure of the residence. The firm geography is an aesthetic feature and serves a functional purpose, providing space to swim laps and play as the situation demands.

The dark, unusual texture of the walls surrounding the pool is balanced by the light, sandy colour of the coping tiles and surrounding paving. These crisp tiles continue into the pool, giving the water a sparkling, vibrant blue that stands out as a focal feature of the courtyard.

Offset in one corner of the yard, a spa breaks up the mass of pool water. Subtly lit from beneath, this clever positional placement ensures that the spa itself doesn't impose on the yard space.

Extensive glazing to the rear of the house provides a strong and integral connection to the interior of the home, as well as the family's open plan kitchen, living and dining room. As such, the pool and nearby alfresco dining area become an extension of the interior, while the elegant, conscientious design is a visual highlight that enhances both spaces.

Photography by: Patrick Redmond

A restrained palette balances rich materials with simple colours to create a dialogue between the pool, the pool surrounds and the home.

residence.

Subiaco

About

Evan Sommerville qualified in South Africa with
a diploma in landscape technology. Throughout
his career he has worked on many award winning
commercial and residential landscape projects
from Brisbane to Perth.

His practice, Exhibit Green, was founded in
2001 with a view towards providing a premium
boutique landscape architectural service
to discerning clients who wanted a unique
and distinctly different approach to garden
architecture. Exhibit Green has a solid grounding
in all aspects of commercial and residential
design, always striving for excellence in client
service and satisfaction. Their strong focus on
natural materials, bold architectural form and
simple elemental design has allowed them to
create an eclectic and distinctive style.

Exhibit Green Design Studio
Perth, Western Australia,
Brisbane, Queensland, AUSTRALIA
T: +61 403 778 878
www.exhibitgreen.com.au

Incorporating some of the owner's existing art pieces into the new landscape has injected personality into the garden. A wood carving called 'Boris' and a large steel seahorse serve as unique and fun garden features.

Subiaco Residence

With its hint of industrial design, this minimal contemporary garden has an edge. Fully embracing the large block, there is an intimacy to this outdoor environment that is achieved through a strong focus on transitional and linked spaces, with all elements flowing together with unexpected ease to bring warmth and depth.

The residence is situated in an extremely well vegetated suburb with an abundance of well-planted and leafy avenues. This lush, full backdrop is diligently replicated within this landscape with colourful flowering trees, shrubs and strappy leafed ground covers. The deep purple of the Prunus nigra provides a stark contrast to the off-form white concrete wall of the pool.

Upon entering the garden through the arbor, there is a natural progression to the pool and front door, with a modified deck linking the garden to the lower storey of the home and interior dining areas. All the feature spaces are integrated into one engaging, functional landscape, ensuring that every part of the design is utilised to its maximum potential.

Pale shades of pink and purple run through the feature Kimberley Sandstone paving, an element that is evocative of the tiles used throughout the iconic Federation Square in Melbourne, Australia. The gentle warmth of this paving serves to soften the hardscaped spaces and integrates well with the colour tones of the softscape planting.

White blooms dotted throughout the garden serve as a magnificent background for the crisp pool frame while in flower. A selection of Crepe myrtles and Manchurian pears provide further screening, while ground covers such as Spider lilies, Crinums and Clivias fill the understorey, drawing in further colour and texture.

There is a strong sense of interconnectedness that permeates the new garden. The elemental and architectural design focuses on individual spaces that grow out from key points, such as the pool, the courtyard, and the entrance. The industrial overtones, achieved with the use of concrete and timber, are balanced by the relaxed warmth of the overall theme.

Photography by: Duncan Barnes and Evan Sommerville

The garden's design is sympathetic to the heritage home it surrounds, yet avoids an attempt at recreating an ungainly country garden. The dedicated spaces and warmth of the aesthetics tie the garden to the home, but with a clean simplicity behind them to give it a modern and unique edge.

Kerlin

residence.

About

When Doug Myers designed and built his first
landscape in 1994, he sought to create something
beautiful; something that would stand the test of time.
Today, nearly twenty years later, Doug and the team
at Fernhill Landscapes strive to improve upon every
single project, creating landscapes of distinct
vision and lasting value.

Doug is a certified member of the Association of
Professional Landscape Designers and a graduate
of Shippensburg University. Informed by extensive
travel not only throughout the USA, but worldwide, his
design work has received numerous state, national and
international awards.

Fernhill Landscapes
42 N. Decatur Street
Strasburg, Pennsylvania 17579, UNITED STATES OF AMERICA
T: +1 717 687 9399
www.fernhilllandscapes.com

The high design of this garden belies its comfort. Bold sculptural forms give way to comfortable, relaxed spaces that are perfect for entertaining.

Kerlin Residence

A minimal hint of sculptural form weaves throughout this series of contemporary garden rooms. As the exterior extension of an updated Colonial residence, the subtle but considered arrangement of landscape materials gives the garden form and is balanced by a sophisticated plant scheme that will mature elegantly.

Sitting at the rear of a suburban block, a strong connection has been formed between house and garden, with the relaxed and contemporary style of the interior leading out into the garden, forming an ideal space for relaxation and alfresco dining.

A secondary entry point is found off the driveway. Access is granted via a Spanish cedar gate, which is supported by powder coated rails and decorated with black brass knobs and hinges. This minimal appearance, while attractive in its own right, serves to complement the nearby pergola, located in the lower garden area. It is within this space that the dining area is nestled, surrounded by a low wall that is capped with cast architectural concrete. A recessed space houses the client's grill, offering a plate up space perfect for casual barbecues. Meanwhile, located closer to the house is a small bar table with chairs; a great spot for breakfast.

The garden is divided, both visually and practically, by a large central wall, which is balanced on one side by a gas fireplace and a water feature wall on the other. Framed by a block of architectural concrete, the hearth also features a cantilevered chimney. Further, a switch is provided to easily start the fire and reduce the workload, even for the most spontaneous of outdoor occasions.

The opposite side of the wall bears a tranquil water feature, cool and calm. A perfectly reflective sheet of water flows over Brazillian slate tiles and spills over into the pool below. The subtle sound of running water mitigates the sound of traffic, while the cool and inviting water creates an atmosphere of tranquility.

Hicksii Yew hedging is placed along the driveway edge of the dining space. Over time, this element will mature and grow to envelop the dining area itself and eclipse the view of the driveway. Meanwhile, the adjacent edge of the garden is defined by three Honey Locusts planted in front of a hedge of 'Manhattan' Euyonomus. The two plants will eventually provide an organic hierarchy, creating a linear window between the canopy of the Locust and the hedge of the Euyonomus.

Traditional devices and the balance of classical garden design find a new context in this modern outdoor space. Sculptural and architectural lines created both by plant and hardscaped elements give this outdoor environment a sublime quality with dramatic impact.

Photography by: Doug Myers

The plantscape matches the architectural theme with striking, bold lines and a range of textural layers.

Lee **residence.**

Fernhill Landscapes
42 N. Decatur Street
Strasburg, Pennsylvania 17579, UNITED STATES OF AMERICA
T: +1 717 687 9399
www.fernhilllandscapes.com

This garden is an exercise in equilibrium: balancing contemporary and traditional, East and West and organic and structured, it forms a perfect transition between a historical home and an artisan's studio.

Lee Residence

This beautiful, organic landscape embodies a subtle Eastern philosophy alongside contemporary European principles in a tribute to commitment and ownership of space. Installed over a period of eight years, the New Romantic style garden sits between an historic home and a converted barn, the latter of which serves as a pottery and jewellery studio, and features a Koi pond, an alfresco dining space and a viewing platform.

This contemplative, transitional garden forms a bridge between the home and work studio, with the progression between the two leading through free flowering plantings on one side, and a more structured Koi and Lotus Garden on the other. Brick terraces laid against the studio and main house create a natural flow between the traditional architecture of the buildings and the more organic features of the garden.

In addition to the main pathway between home and workspace, two additional paths lead ponderously through the garden, allowing for closer views of the plantings. The plant scheme was strongly influenced by Dutchman Piet Odoulf, where colour is of secondary importance and the primary focus is on the shapes of the grass and flower heads. As such, flowers and grasses with contrasting form are consistently used throughout the design.

Overall, this garden exhibits a respect for traditional design, readily embracing the existing architecture of the historical property. Despite this, the design embellishes upon classic ideas and forms with more modern alternatives.

Photography by: Doug Myers

A subtle hint of Eastern design can be seen in the balance of the garden and the conceptualisation of the space as a tranquil, reflective area to bridge two discrete and functional elements.

Sterling
garden.

Fernhill Landscapes
42 N. Decatur Street
Strasburg, Pennsylvania 17579, UNITED STATES OF AMERICA
T: +1 717 687 9399
www.fernhilllandscapes.com

Matching an iconic mid-century architectural home with a timeless and verdant geometric garden design, this interior courtyard is a stunning and tranquil outdoor room.

Sterling Garden

Blending elegant contemporary forms with lush plantings, the Sterling garden is a sensory experience that combines striking visuals with a range of rich textures and the soothing, constant presence of water. Occupying the interior courtyard of a house designed in 1948 by Architect Cliff May, this garden complements the mid century home and provides a new visual feature within.

With an aesthetic that is just as visually striking from within the home as it is from inside the courtyard, there is a clear sculptural quality to this design. Hardscape materials characterise simple, geometric forms, while the planting palette emphasises form over colour to achieve a thoroughly modern aesthetic. The courtyard itself is presented as a graphic composition of space, hardscape and planting defined by stones and greenery.

Rectangular slabs of Teakwood flagstone form the bulk of the ground surface and are framed by Mexican beach pebbles, accentuating the patterns of the flagstone. The outside perimeter of these pebbles is contained by low profile edging.

Central to this design is its water feature. Water flows from a custom made copper bowl into the attractive L-shaped pond, constructed of pressure treated wood with a custom, box liner insert. The subtle sound of water flowing combines with the gentle, reflective quality of the water itself to create an atmosphere of relaxation.

Well considered and simple, this design is timeless. The sculptural quality complements the modern feel of the home and creates a sublime and dramatic view from both inside the courtyard and the home itself.

While colour was a secondary concern in the planting, it was nonetheless a considered factor, with the subtle greens bursting occasionally against gentle white flowers to accentuate the simple geometric forms of the design. Boxwoods, Black Bamboo and Ornamental Grasses contrast dramatically with the hardscape to soften the garden's aesthetic.

Photography by: Doug Myers

Trailfinders Australian Garden
presented by
fleming's.

About

As a third generation nurseryman, Wes Fleming was 'born and bred' growing trees. The family business, Fleming's Nurseries, was established in the early 1920's and is now Australia's leading grower and wholesaler of deciduous fruiting and ornamental trees and shrubs to retail garden centres, urban development, landscapers and local government.

In 2004, Wes' vision of placing the Australian horticulture industry on the world stage was realised with the first ever Australian show garden to be exhibited at the prestigious Chelsea Flower Show in London. Since then, Wes has initiated, project managed and sponsored seven more trips to Chelsea, which have been awarded prestigious 'Silver-Gilt' and 'Gold' medals.

Fleming's Nurseries
PO Box 1
Monbulk, Victoria 3793, AUSTRALIA
T: +61 3 9756 6105
www.flemings.com.au

Awarded the Silver Gilt Medal, the design is a tribute to cutting edge landscape design, both in Australia and worldwide.

Trailfinders Australian Garden presented by Fleming's

The Trailfinders Australian Garden, designed by Jason Hodges and implemented at the Chelsea Flower Show, employs an eclectic plant palette and a quintessentially Australian layout.

Making the Trailfinders garden possible was a team of 12 Aussies using 38 tonnes of tools, equipment, materials and plants sourced both locally and abroad. Built over 17 days, what was once a bare stretch of grass became a lush garden retreat. This feat of design, landscaping, engineering and construction was facilitated by Wes Fleming, the team leader.

The garden boasts a number of must-have fixtures of Australian outdoor living. A plunge pool and outdoor deck are classic inclusions, while the more luxurious additions of an outdoor shower and bath sit nearby. A barbecue and pizza oven speak to the Australian tradition of outdoor entertaining, while a gas fireplace serves to complete the stunning outdoor room.

The textural range of the garden evokes elegant, inner-city Australia as easily as it suggests the raw, exposed rural elements of the country. The rich timber and rusted corrugated iron are laid alongside sandstone to suggest the untamed outback, yet the restrained contemporary articulation and clean, sleek finishes suggest a stylish urban garden.

Photography by: Josh Whitby

The planting scheme employs species both native and introduced that have become synonymous with cutting-edge Australian landscaping. Though diverse, the planted spaces are nonetheless restrained, introducing only greens, dull reds and whites to balance the materiality of the garden.

balmoral.

About

Formed Gardens is a small, passionate team of
landscape architects, designers and contractors
with over 10 years experience.

Our projects range from small courtyards and
gardens, to pools and large scale, multi unit
developments. Our focus is on getting the spaces
right and seeing projects built.

Formed Gardens is committed to producing high
quality gardens and landscapes that will enhance your
lifestyle, bring your vision to life, and last the tests of
time. 'If it's outside, we can build it for you'.

Formed Gardens
16 South Creek Road
Collaroy, New South Wales 2097, AUSTRALIA
T: +61 2 9982 5774
www.formedgardens.com.au

It was by working closely with the architects and builders that Formed Gardens were able to create a garden that so perfectly enhances the home it accompanies.

Balmoral

This subtle outdoor room by the team at Formed Gardens accentuates the contemporary architecture of the new build home it frames, blending old and new with a subtle Asian theme that is informed by the existing artwork of the owners.

The garden is thoroughly modern in layout and form. Its large and generous spaces are defined by the building lines and architecture of the home and simultaneously reflect the house's aesthetics. While balancing the wholly structured composition of the building, there is an organic aspect to this landscape design, with recycled sandstone and timber softened by massed plantings and ponds that give contrast and depth.

Water plays an integral role in tying the garden together. Reflections and views from the pool, ponds and water bowls dotted throughout the site are a gentle, natural feature that serve as a strong thematic link throughout the garden. A blend of recycled sandstone and imported stone forms much of the hardscaping, with the nearby timber providing a beautiful textural contrast.

The planting comprises a mix of local natives, accents and sub-tropical species that respond to the many micro-climates within the large site. In particular, massed native grasses and shrubs are used for impact and drama in the sheltered areas around the building. Boundary fences were painted with a black stain to enhance the impact of the plants.

Photography by: Steve Carrol - 'Naig Vision'

Resplendent in its simplicity, this garden complements the architecture of the new building without overpowering it.

Bungan
beach.

Formed Gardens
16 South Creek Road
Collaroy, New South Wales 2097, AUSTRALIA
T: +61 2 9982 5774
www.formedgardens.com.au

Raw finishes and a selection of hardy,
textural and attractive materials give
this simple garden unique character.

Bungan Beach

The stunning outlook from this cliff-top site is beautifully framed by this simple garden. A series of stepped terraces, articulated in greyed timbers and ballast sandstone, address the challenges of the sloping site and give way to borrowed landscape and an incredible view.

The white, architecturally designed residence on the cliff face of Bungan Beach in New South Wales deserved a beautiful garden, both as a visual complement to the home itself and to provide practical, inviting spaces for the family to live and play in outdoors. By working in conjunction with a team of architects and builders, the resulting wooden terraces utilise angled boundary and building lines to take full advantage of the ocean context, and give way to an integral lawn area and a large pool.

Matching the simple yet evocative architecture of the home, the garden's design is contemporary, minimalistic and quintessentially coastal. The combination of timber faded to a natural and weathered grey, dry stone walling and seaward planting crafts a visual effect that the block naturally progresses from home to beach.

The subtle material palette, built on a strong base of recycled sandstone, reflects and complements the landscape. A selection of hardy coastal plants produce grey-green tones and organic shapes that blend well with the grey hardwood timber decking and finished concrete. The generous array of spaces ensures that there is room for every possible outdoor activity for every family member in the garden. Lawn areas provide a place for kids to frolic, while a casual outdoor entertaining area overlooks everything and is a perfect place to relax alone or with friends.

Plants:

Coastal Rosemary – Westringia fruticosa
Agave – Agave attenuata
Chalk Sticks – Senecio mandraliscae
Crassula - Crassula
Frangi Pani (Plumeria Rubra)
Mexican Lily (Beschorneria Yuccoides)

Photography by: Steve Carrol - 'Naig Vision'

The simple, natural material palette is matched by a selection of hardy coastal plants that offer grey-green tones and organic shapes. Transplanted frangipani trees and a subtlety of tones in both the material and planted palette lend elegance and approachability to the design.

Project 56

surrey.

About

Formed in 1998 and based in Fulham, south-west London, Garden Builders specialises in the design and construction of private domestic gardens, both in the UK and overseas. In addition, they also work for a variety of established and up-and-coming landscape architects and designers to interpret their designs and create truly beautiful gardens for their clients.

The Garden Builders have gained a solid reputation within the industry for producing well-constructed gardens with a keen eye for detail, as well as running well-managed schemes that are completed within budget and on time in truly inspirational form.

Garden Builders
259 Munster Road
Fulham, London SW6 6BW, UNITED KINGDOM
T: +44 20 7381 8002
www.gardenbuilders.co.uk

There is a sense of wonder and joy that tugs at even the most serious adults who enter this garden. Bright colours, rich textures, secret places to hide and a myriad things on which to swing and climb inspire visitors to indulge.

Project 56 Surrey

Set within a large private garden in Surrey, UK, this delightfully colourful play area is every child's dream backyard. Designed in-house by Jacek Wac and Neil Dunster of Garden Builders and constructed by their team, this project was a true labor of love, resulting in a spectacular private playground.

The site itself posed a few challenges. The original ground level had an apreciable slope and was therefore not ideal for the contemporary play space that the owners had in mind. Additionally, a yew edging had to be retained in the new design. By levelling the garden, rubber-paved surfaces could be laid to add safety for the children, while the yew edging works in the garden's favour by enclosing and warming the space, lending the feeling of a private playground sanctuary.

The garden has been filled with everything a child could ever dream of in a play space. The rubber paving is a soft, colourful and interestingly textured surface. In addition, there is absolutely no shortage of activities, with slides, trampolines, a sand pit, tunnels, swings, a climbing frame, monkey bars and a tornado spinner all included, many of which were also custom-designed and built for this design.

The planting is lush and architectural, paired thematically to the hardscaped space. Large tree ferns and herbaceous perennials provide instant structure and dynamic change throughout the seasons, balanced by a range of low grasses that fill the negative space.

The fun, functional environment that Garden Builders created is a charming and inspirational playground, and one that makes visitors wish they were six years old again.

Photography by: Jacek Wac

The Surrey Garden was announced as the 'Special Feature' Category Winner at the prestigious Association of Professional Landscaper Awards in 2011.

San Francisco

residence.

About

Lutsko Associates are dedicated to high quality, forward thinking landscape design. Our work explores and expresses relationships between people and the environment. We employ a rigorous design process to create thoughtful and meaningful landscapes with a sound theoretical base.

Headed by Ron Lutsko, Jr., principal and founder, the firm consists of nine associates, each bringing a unique background to projects. Since the founding of the firm in San Francisco in 1981, Lutsko Associates now works on projects throughout the world.

Lutsko Associates
2815 18th Street
San Francisco, California 94110, UNITED STATES OF AMERICA
T: +1 415 920 2800
www.lutskoassociates.com

Each area is distinct in form and quality, the first of which is both light filled and private. Translucent glass allows a subtle, diffused light into the garden, and provides shadowy hints of shapes and forms within the next space.

San Francisco Residence

Located in the Pacific Heights district of San Francisco, this urban residential garden takes full advantage of a small space with three discretely landscaped sections, each enclosed and rigorously defined by both architectural and planted edges. While the space can be appreciated from the upper levels of the house, it is best experienced from within as an intimate and connected series of restful courtyards around the home.

Built as a complement to a contemporary-designed residence built in the early 90s, the garden represents a graphic and textural composition, juxtaposing hardscaped space, materiality and planting. Drawing a sense of San Francisco's urban fabric onto the site, the garden frames views to the city, the bay and Alcatraz Island in the distance.

A variety of finishes define the edges of the garden, including translucent glass, hand-trowled plaster, a curved bronze wall and planted areas. Clipped hedges fit within the structure of a steel frame to form the walls between each 'room'.

The second room, perhaps the boldest space, is dominated by the most dramatic element of the garden - a large, curved wall made of bronze. Water cascades from a slot in this wall into a basin cut into the paving beneath, producing an impressive and eye-catching water feature.

The third garden space frames a stunning view of San Francisco, the bay, and the Trans-America building through an open window, which is cut into a semi-translucent wall. The reeded glass panels, which are layered over the Beaux-

Arts balustrade of the neighbouring property, acknowledge the pastiche of the city and make reference to the changing styles of architecture over time. A lemon tree, highlighted against a plaster wall, is aligned with the garden's axial view.

This garden is given an architectural edge and a sense of place and time thanks to its bold material palette. Light limestone paving seems to glow beneath the San Francisco fog. A restrained planting scheme in combination with bands of wooly thyme and dark granite highlight form over colour, while textural foliage contrasts well with the materiality of the space. This garden evolves naturally from the architecture of the residence, unfolding into a dynamic series of beautiful environments.

Once inside this garden, there is a palpable sensation of intimate enclosure and an exciting journey through the distinct spaces.

Photography by: Marion Brenner

design.
A European

A European Design

Innovative and original both in design and styling, Maison Design highlights some stunning products that bring a touch of European chic to any garden space. Crafting creative, quality driven works of art, Maison seeks to offer durable, beautiful feature products for use both inside and outdoors. Of particular note are the innovative products by Q Design, a step forward in the evolution of creative possibility.

Light features create a stunning and dynamic focal point that can change the entire mood of an outdoor space. The dramatic silhouette of a windblown tree, as seen on the previous page, lends this small courtyard a romantic, intimate atmosphere that only becomes more theatrical as evening descends. Maison offers quality weather-proof LED light features for inside and out, made to order in a variety of designs, metals and finishes.

Quality paving can elevate and transform a garden. Designer paving products from Maison are available in a variety of styles, patterns and designs and can serve as wall cladding, pool coping or ground cover. Sandstone pavers are a classic garden product, and are an attractive way to hint at an exotic escape even in a limited space.

Whether large or small, classic or modern, sculptures are an integral and often overlooked element of a successful outdoor space. Maison offers a range of custom designed and fabricated large and small scale sculptural works. Available in a variety of metals and finishes including aged rust, powder coated aluminium, stainless steel and MDF, the leaves pictured here are particularly effective. Modern without being overwhelming and subtly integrating into any garden style, these subtle notes offer a 'less is more' approach to decorative furnishing.

Sculpted wall panels, available in Maison's unique reconstituted sandstone, are contemporary carved and moulded acoustic wall cladding panels. These offer a unique way to create a striking visual feature that is both minimal and impacting.

Q Designs are versatile and can be easily implemented as an attractive feature on a rendered wall, or used to screen off or partition part of your garden. They should reflect the unique style and character of the home and garden they sit within, and are available in the same extensive range of metals and finishes as the sculptures mentioned above.

Offering a versatile range of products, Maison's beautiful range of highly designed and crafted outdoor products will be able to supply a feature that compliments and contrasts with your existing colour palette or to enhance your new garden design.

Maison Design
57 Rundle Street East
Kent Town, South Australia 5067, AUSTRALIA
T: +61 8 8363 9266
www.maisondesign.com.au

Maison offers the following advice: "Don't overcomplicate. Keeping things simple is the best way to ensure artwork stands out in your garden design."

armadale.

About

Nathan Burkett's bold style and eye for detail results
in stunning individual gardens that respond brilliantly
to site and brief. Having worked for a number of years
under highly acclaimed landscape designer Robert
Boyle, Nathan brings with him a wealth of experience
in detailed construction and approaches each of his
projects with a sound understanding of both design
and implementation.

Nathan began his own practice, Nathan Burkett Design,
in 2004, and has worked on many of Australia's finest
gardens. He seeks excellence in his designs, sourcing
only the best materials internationally. With many
accolades under his belt, Nathan won the prestigious
Allan Correy award for design excellence in 2010,
the Abode Garden of the Year award in 2011 and
has a project featured in the 2012 Rotary Open
Garden Scheme.

Nathan Burkett Design
Ringwood, Victoria 3134, AUSTRALIA
T: +61 3 9095 8344
www.nathanburkett.com.au

The inclusion of feature lighting allows this garden to be admired at any time of the day or night, making this the true centrepiece of the property.

Armadale

Blending seamlessly from indoors to out, this luxurious landscape by Nathan Burkett Design sets the benchmark for contemporary outdoor living. With a formal elegance, the area is perfect for entertaining friends and family on special occasions. Accent lighting, hand-made features and a glorious pool make this the ultimate outdoor entertainment facility.

Chic and simple landscaping at the front of the property provides just the right amount of adornment for this contemporary home, with sleek flooring and simple, feature lit trees setting the tone for what lies ahead. A floating travertine pathway carries visitors to the intriguing front gate, beyond which Nathan's sophisticated creation continues to unfold.

It is often the pool that becomes the hero of a landscape design. However, while the extensive lap pool is certainly stunning as it glistens in the sun and creates a spectacular effect on the house's white exterior, a harmonious balance has been achieved in this area between hard, soft and fluid elements.

Surrounded by bluestone paving and a hand cut travertine floating seat, the garden is given that keen contemporary edge. To juxtapose this however, a timber screen with a picture window allows visual access to the soft scape behind, incorporating a subtle, stainless steel water feature to add warmth and character. Consistent with the design at the front of the property, dark screening provides a backdrop against which the plants can

visually pop. With a large alfresco area that is built into the roofline of the home, the expansive exterior dining space makes for an excellent alternative to the traditional family dinner table.

Despite the irregular shape of the block itself, the design cleverly accommodates for all the essentials while emphasising a sense of space and depth. Through a variety of materials, colours and textures, the garden also retains character and personality, avoiding the cold and pretentious stereotype associated with contemporary design.

Careful planning and attention to detail have come together nicely in this outstanding design, culminating in a garden that has a unique vibe of class and simplicity.

brighton.

Nathan Burkett Design
Ringwood, Victoria 3134, AUSTRALIA
T: +61 3 9095 8344
www.nathanburkett.com.au

Visual depth is created with elegant, layered planter boxes and a range of material textures.

Brighton

Constructed within a tight space at the front of a magnificent Brighton house, this architectural landscape is evidence of what is achievable with a bit of imagination. Serving as a testament to the versatility of the landscape trade, this garden is a great example of how attention to design in a small space can achieve big things.

A lack of space to the rear of the property created a need for the landscaped elements to appear at the front of the site. This negotiation presented quite a challenge to Nathan and his team, who then conceptualised a space saving design that incorporated a pool, spa, alfresco area and private terrace, all in a plan that would be a perfect complement to the home.

Planter boxes line the pool to bring garden and water together. The pool is the hero of the space, wrapping around a large planter box that features a stunning Magnolia that is lit from below. Not only does this feature provide visual interest, but it acts as an alternative pool fence. In addition, it defines the pool's main access point next to the spa from the more private entry of the master suite.

A timber deck extends from the home's living area. This transitional space is utilised as an alfresco dining and entertainment area, and is made cosy and private by the adjacent garden.

The charcoal and white colour palette of the landscape echoes that of the residence. Rich timber tones and bright green plants give the entire space a feeling of balanced, full liveliness. The home's modern aesthetic is reflected in the sharp lines of the landscape and pool, with the featured plants being those that soften the space.

Concealed by high walls, this garden is afforded privacy despite being located close to the street.

Photography by: Urban Angles Photography

Caulfield
north.

Nathan Burkett Design
Ringwood, Victoria 3134, AUSTRALIA
T: +61 3 9095 8344
www.nathanburkett.com.au

Careful planning of the site layout was integral to the strength of the design. The swimming pool was positioned first, in the north east corner of the block where existing boundary walls would make a functional pool fence.

Caulfield North

Simple and serene, this elegant landscape is open, fresh and functional, but restrained design and unyielding craftsmanship offer an intimacy and warmth that create a sense of isolation and privacy. Ideal for a young family and undeniably striking, this garden is the result of entirely trusting the integrity of the designer.

The front space posed an initial challenge, with a two-metre rise from path to entrance making it difficult to incorporate unobtrusive access to the house. In response, the garden has been decorated with large polished concrete slabs that appear as if stacked on top of one another, making the transition from the footpath to the door a strong design element rather than simply a clumsy set of stairs.

The planting is understated throughout the design, but is particularly effective in front of the striking contemporary façade. It becomes a softening vertical element that balances the bold lines of the house and further eases the transition of the slope. The tiered design and the gentle integration of materials between the front garden to the house creates a logical transition from the house to the rear garden.

Modest planting in the lawn area turns a pedestrian space into another important element of the expansive retreat. Here, everything is gently emphasized by subtle lighting, which works to draw out features of the garden. A sheltered outdoor entertaining area offers an ideal transition from the interior to the exterior space and a portal to the garden.

Rigorous design and unyielding attention to detail has resulted in this natural progression of spaces that connects seamlessly to a beautiful modern family home. It is rare that designers have free reign on a project, but in the hands of Nathan Burkett Design the result is a modest, elegant outdoor space perfectly suited to family life.

Photography by: Urban Angles Photography

Elevated to renew the levels and layering of the design, the cool white of the tiles, the sandier deck and the glistening pool are balanced by warm timber highlights.

sorrento.

Nathan Burkett Design
Ringwood, Victoria 3134, AUSTRALIA
T: +61 3 9095 8344
www.nathanburkett.com.au

The impact of this space is created not in dramatic statements but in subtle, detailed inclusions like the simple pool-side water feature.

Sorrento

Surrounded by greenery, this elegant and angular landscape design seems to gently cut into the bush, carving straight lines naturally into the delimiting shrubbery. A subtle beach house theme and a functional pool complete this graceful garden.

Upon exiting the house, one is greeted by the warmth of a classic timber deck. The Ironbark deck is traditional, but the use of wharf style stainless steel screws subtly references the beachside nature of the property and creates a point of difference to the deck. Surrounded by low limestone walls at seating height, this is an intimate space that is subtly separated from the rest of the garden. Connection is maintained, however, by the extensive use of frameless glass fencing, which ensures pool safety while minimising the visual barrier.

The plunge pool is ideally suited to this garden. It is long enough to swim laps and features a submerged paved swimout, perfect as a play space for young children. Stainless steel tubes serve as a subtle, stylish water feature, gently and consistently pouring into the pool. Honey limestone paving surrounding the pool is a warm, beachy colour, complemented by the teak garden furniture that features throughout.

Tall trees surrounding the property provide a shield from neighbours and give the garden a private, protected feeling. This is further enhanced by the Ficus Hilli 'Flash' hedge that runs the length of the pool. Planting, though minimal, is effective, softening the sharp rectangles of the garden. A lawn space is provided as a play area or simply a place to relax. A raised garden bed subtly frames this space, while Agave attenuata are a subtle low maintenance underplant to the taller trees.

Everything in this garden highlights the juncture of angles, a pleasing design feature that requires an eye for detail and expert craftsmanship to ensure crisp lines and clearly defined outdoor rooms. Vertical layers and jutting horizontal spaces combine in an enclosed and private beach house garden that offers something to every visitor of the space.

Photography by: Kristen Burkett

Frameless glass ensures that the pool is safe without breaking up the visual flow, giving the garden depth and a sense of space.

Dalkeith
residence.

About

Newforms Landscape Architecture is a vibrant and dynamic team, practicing in the field of Landscape Architecture. With a focus on cutting edge design, Newforms prides itself on its creative, unique, intuitive and sustainable solutions to the design challenges that are presented by the contemporary urban and natural Australian environments.

Newforms Landscape Architecture was founded in 2001 by Directors Matt Huxtable BLArch.(hons) and Ryan Healy BLArch, who met whilst studying at the University of Western Australia.

Matt Huxtable, Newforms Director

Newforms Landscape Architecture
Unit 4 - 11 Milson Place
O'Connor, Western Australia 6163, AUSTRALIA
T: +61 8 9331 7911
www.newforms.com.au

The garden has an almost surreal aspect when viewed from inside, especially at night when lit.

Dalkeith Residence

Encompassing two distinct spaces, this peaceful, elegant garden moves through a large courtyard and culminates in a sunken end garden. Stylish and modern, the garden begins with an expansive open area that is framed by a stainless steel arbour. This then leads into a recessed space that gives depth and tranquility to the design.

Flanked on three sides by the residence, this inner courtyard provides stunning focal points for many areas of the interior. The design plays on perspective and illusion, adding highlights that the eye can glide over and points at which the eyes naturally come to rest. The extensive glazing that frames the garden turns the outdoor space into a dynamic feature, a 'living painting' that draws on Japanese landscape and garden design to emphasise the importance of careful positioning and composition.

As the first space that visitors enter upon leaving the house, the courtyard is impressive in its simplicity. The arbour, articulated in steel, is a light structure with minimal beam size. A gentle arc in the frame's shape serves to soften the rigid geometry of the hardscaping beneath it. Selected for its durability, the steel frame adds an interesting contrast to the more earthy, textural materials used in the adjoining garden. The stainless steel itself also serves as a beautiful juxtaposition to the bright green foliage of the grape vines, transplanted from their original locations to work in the new spatial composition.

Meanwhile, the sunken garden is, by design, heavily structured and yet simple. A long Koi pond reinforces perspective lines from the house, while an L-shaped bench seat allows for comfortable, quiet conversation. The exaggerated perspective is reinforced by the installation of two large Frangipani trees, the larger of which is planted towards the view from the inside, while the smaller sits behind it.

A minimal use of plant types and considered species selection throughout the yard was used as a means of ensuring water efficiency and low maintenance. A range of Succulents introduces an interesting contrast to the Frangipanis' colours, textures and forms without compromising the garden's ease of use.

Natural limestone is used in the hardscaped spaces as a durable, practical base and is balanced by natural slate mulch in the gardens. This represents another low maintenance offering, which, in turn, also provides an unusual texture within the garden composition.

The garden's focal water feature represents a 'mirror' for the residence, as its travertine marble cladding is used as internal flooring within the house. The parapet wall located behind this feature is plain, and painted 'cobar' red, contrasting against the Frangipani trees without creating a visual distraction from the water.

Though the garden is thoroughly contemporary, a hint of classic style creeps in: beneath the grapes, the exposed aggregate paving throughout the courtyard is a reference to the original terrazzo found inside the 1930s home.

Duncraig
road.

About

Outside In specializes in Landscape Architectural Design and Construction. After 12 years in operation, the company has emerged as a leader in innovative landscape design and implementation. With an in-house staff that consists of a principal project manager, a landscape designer, landscape architects, sales and administrative staff and a network of professional and highly qualified tradespeople, Outside In will see a project from beginning to end, providing a stunning solution to any landscaped space.

The firm believes that beautiful landscapes are those that facilitate a peaceful co-existence between the home and the outdoor space, a lifestyle choice that enhances the home.

Outside In
370a Canning Highway
Como, Western Australia 6152, AUSTRALIA
T: +61 8 9450 4922
www.outsidein.net.au

By raising the entire pool structure from the ground, what was initially only a functional pool became a stunning water feature, turning a practical but visually void feature into an aesthetic pleasure.

Duncraig Road

This mind-blowing home deserved a garden with serious wow factor to serve as an exterior entertainment and family area. This polished and well balanced garden certainly says "wow", but it is a subtle, insistent reminder of the natural environment that truly makes this an inspiring outdoor space.

The planted areas on the front verge are a perfect complement to the journey toward the house. A range of Australian natives including Red Kangaroo Paws and various Dianellas create a low maintenance and well-conceived garden.

Central to the front garden is the pool. Though it takes up considerable space, it doesn't overwhelm the design or detract from the pleasure of the alfresco dining area it frames. By raising the entire pool structure from the ground, what was initially only a functional pool became a stunning water feature, turning a practical but visually void feature into an aesthetic pleasure. The unique shape of the pool means it sits like a gem against the front boundary. An outdoor shower nearby ensures that pool water need never be tracked through the house.

At the rear of the property, space was set aside for a much-desired herb and vegetable garden with a short avenue of fruit trees. This quiet retreat from the grandiose entertaining space provides a pleasant balance to the garden.

The design takes into account the practical needs of the family. As such, a patch of lawn was included for the trampoline, an addition that adds a touch of down-to-earth fun in this magnificent outdoor space.

Stunning outdoor furniture from the Royal Britannia collection and fun LED ball lights from Outside In that float in the pool bring the design together, uniting the interior and exterior and ensuring a logical and interesting flow. Though this garden is exciting, elegant and luxurious, it is the well-considered planting that is the true star, giving the entire property a sense of grounded consideration that the otherwise dramatic design might lack. The wow factor is undeniable in this stunning yard, but the subtleties in the landscaping give this innovative design a timelessness that truly enhances the home.

Plants
Dragon Tree – *Dracaena draco*
Swans Neck Agave – *Agave attenuate*
Blue Mountain Grass – *Festuca glauca*
Dragon Tree – *Dracaena marginata*
Red flowering frangipani – *Apocynaceae, Plumeria rubra*

Photography by: Ron Tan

Though this garden is exciting, elegant and luxurious, it is the well-considered planting that is the true star, giving the entire property a sense of grounded consideration that the otherwise dramatic design might lack.

Los Altos Hills
Infinity Swimming
pool.

About

Having studied Interior Design and Horticulture at the University of Florida, Diane Hayford founded Skyline design studio in 1993. Her background includes 10 years in Architectural and Interior Design in New York City, after which she moved to California and expanded her study of horticulture. As such, her landscape designs combine the sensitivity of architecture, interior design and horticulture with a uniquely creative eye and careful attention to detail.

When not designing daring hillside swimming pools or beautifully detailed carpentry, Diane loves bicycling, dancing, cooking and, of course, gardening! As she herself says, "I find inspiration in everything, from the natural beauty I see on my bike rides to the fantasy world of professional Ballet."

Skyline design studio
4020 Fabian Way - Suite #301
Palo Alto, California 94303, UNITED STATES OF AMERICA
T: +1 650 843 0844
www.skylinedesignstudio.net

This garden, built on a series of levels, commands a spectacular 270° view of the surrounding hills.

Los Altos Hills Infinity Swimming Pool

Effortlessly mirroring the beautifully remodelled home it surrounds, this stunning, contemporary garden offers a collection of entertaining spaces across a number of levels, with each area taking full advantage of the spectacular views of the undulating landscape.

The warm, golden stucco finish of the house is extended into the garden via the various retaining walls, creating a strong link between landscape and home. Aptos Gold flagstone pavers line the patios, while matching flagstones cap the walls.

The rich, dusty colour this provides contrasts well with the luscious green trees within the design, in addition to matching the golden hues of the unfolding Californian scenery.

While the gently sloping block is ideal for capturing the beautiful outlook, the previous garden had a steep and abrupt descent that left little available space. The newly re-terraced garden, on the other hand, steps down gradually, with the differing elevations linking the lower levels with the upper land.

Perhaps this garden's most striking elements are its two functional water features. The double infinity edge pool is both dramatic and prominent; a bold blue slash that cuts into the design. A waterway then connects this swimming pool to a large round spa with curved infinity edges. Italian glass tile mosaics are used on the pool and spa walls, producing a graphic art aesthetic. This feature truly comes alive at night time, with art glass inserts glowing with light and an inviting ambient warmth.

Located in an area where deer frequently roam, the plantings had to be as graze-proof as possible. A succulent garden is laid within the curving bed found below the spa, offering a colourful tapestry when viewed from above. Mediterranean plants such as Rosemary, Cistus and Lavender create a colourful carpet beneath the magnificent Oaks on the hillside below the pool.

Photography by: Diane Hayford

Woodside
garden.

Skyline design studio
4020 Fabian Way - Suite #301
Palo Alto, California 94303, UNITED STATES OF AMERICA
T: +1 650 843 0844
www.skylinedesignstudio.net

Hardscaped form and the organic, chaotic growth of nature harmonise beautifully in this expansive garden retreat.

Woodside Garden

Found on a gently sloping block surrounded by forest in Woodside, California, this naturalistic garden represents a private sanctuary. A subtle Asian theme pervades the lush outdoor space, with numerous focal points included to define and zone the garden. Embracing its forest context and showcasing abundant organic beauty, this landscape design embraces a sense of comfortable progression and balance.

Surrounding a multi-storey house with a broad array of windows, this garden was crafted to be attractive from every angle. The design flows from the front of the property to the rear and emphasises its natural beauty. New hand-hewn stone retaining walls gracefully terrace the sloping site to provide patios spaces. Idaho Quartzite forms the bulk of the hardscape and is punctuated by rectangular pads, with patterns in quartzite, black slate and black pebbles. ·

The plantings within this landscape design provide a range of textures and colours of foliage, with each variation blending well with the verdant, wooded site. Beautiful hand-hewn stone features, including the light pillars and pedestals, create places for artwork and a collection of Bonsai trees, reinforcing the near-Asian theme.

Plants:

Dwarf conifers: Picea "Little Gem"
Japanese Maples – Acer japonicum
American Barberry: Berberis "Crimson Pygmy"
Manzanita: Arctostaphylos "Howard McMinn"
Mahonia lomariifolia

The foyer of the home originally looked out onto a mossy spa and deck. These were removed in the new design to make way for the decorative floating metallic steps, which serve as a point of access from the foyer doors. These then lead down to a path of stepping-stones, which form a charming bridge across a small artificial waterfall.

Photography by: Diane Hayford

Arthritis Research UK
garden.

About

Garden designer Thomas Hoblyn developed his passion
for plants in the West Country, where his family had
lived and farmed for generations. He later went on to
hone his horticultural skills at Hadlow College and the
Royal Botanic Gardens in Kew.

Establishing Thomas Hoblyn Garden Design in 2002
after some years spent abroad, Tom has worked on
commissions as geographically diverse as they are
varied. Since 2006, his practice has designed some
truly outstanding award-winning gardens, with
this year representing his fourth show garden at the
Chelsea Flower Show.

Thomas Hoblyn Garden Design LTD
Mansard House - Low Street
Bury St. Edmunds, Suffolk IP31 1AR, UNITED KINGDOM
T: +44 1359 252056
www.thomashoblyn.com

Subtly embodying a theme of 'rebirth' with a modern take on Renaissance garden design, this garden is an exercise in harmony with nature.

Arthritis Research UK Garden

Arthritis Research UK had used only one word to impart their brief to Thomas Hoblyn: "Rebirth". They desired a garden that would represent the rebirth of their organisation. With this ideal in mind, Hoblyn drew on the techniques and styles of perhaps one of the most influential rebirths in design history, the Renaissance, to inform his design.

Drawing on the rich classicism and formal style of Renaissance period architecture and gardens, this landscape design has a pleasing balance and symmetry. The Renaissance ambition to control nature is gently expressed in clipped Cyprus trees and a complex water feature. By and large however, the ornate decoration has been pared back, lending the outdoor room a more contemporary aesthetic.

The more natural features within the garden contrast against the strict form and balance that is central to the design. A crooked cork oak and rough stone at the perimeter of the garden serve as a reminder that nature cannot be fully tamed.

There are coincidental nods to the work of Arthritis Research UK within this design. While not intentional, these subtle allusions lend themselves to a garden sponsored by the organisation. Raised planter beds, for example, are particularly suited to arthritis sufferers for ease of access. In addition, the planting includes Borage - a plant that produces oils used medicinally for arthritis treatment.

Deconstructing the Renaissance notion of dominion over nature, the central form and structure of this garden is framed by a reminder that nature always has the final word. The elegance of the man made design is enhanced by the layer of beauty the unruliness of nature provides.

Photography by: Gary Takle

Salame

residence.

Vladimir Djurovic Landscape Architecture
Villa Rizk
Broumana, LEBANON
T: +961 4 862 444
www.vladimirdjurovic.com

An extensive, multi-purpose water element delineates the garden space to the front of the home, providing a safe boundary that embraces the usable areas of the garden.

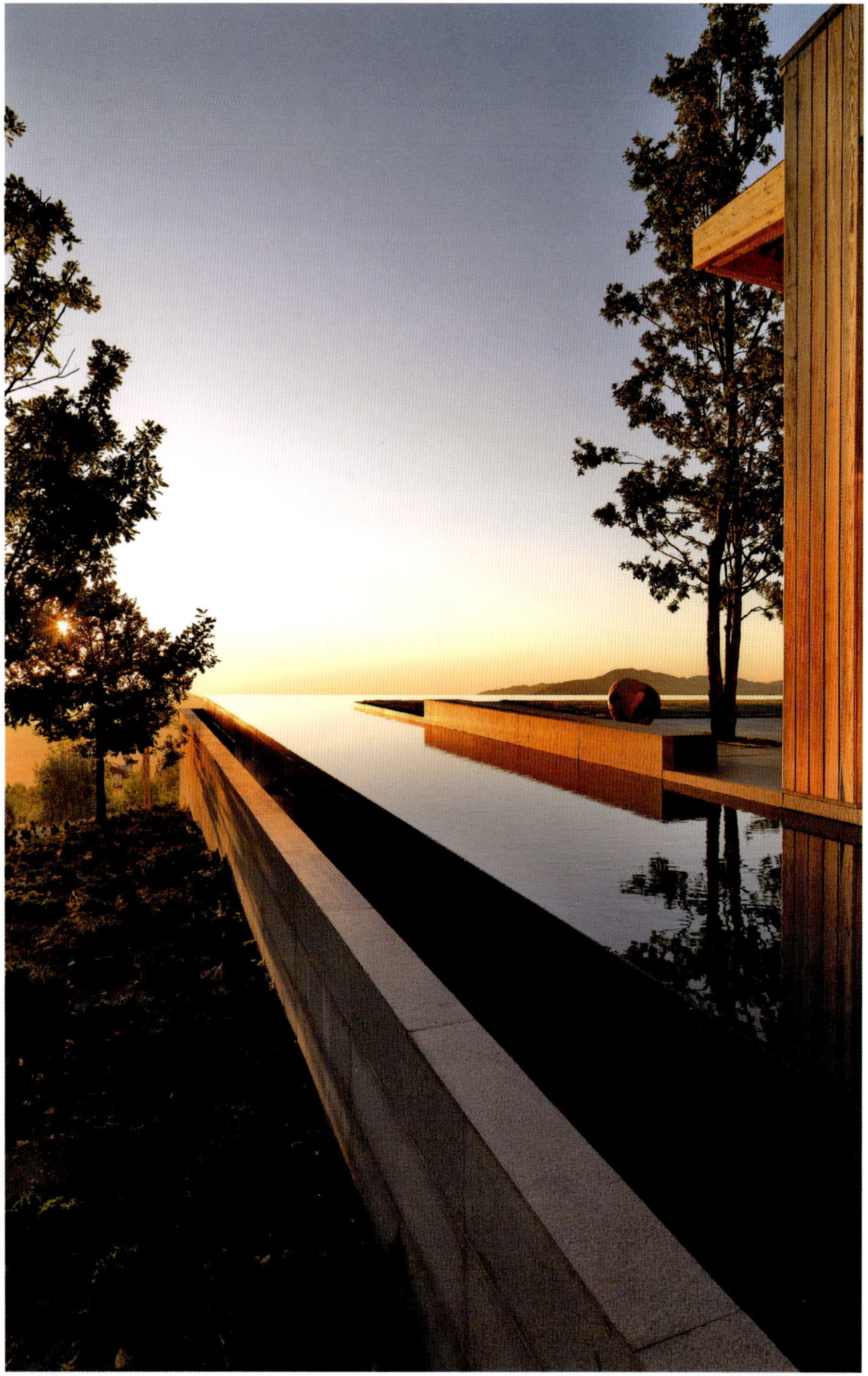

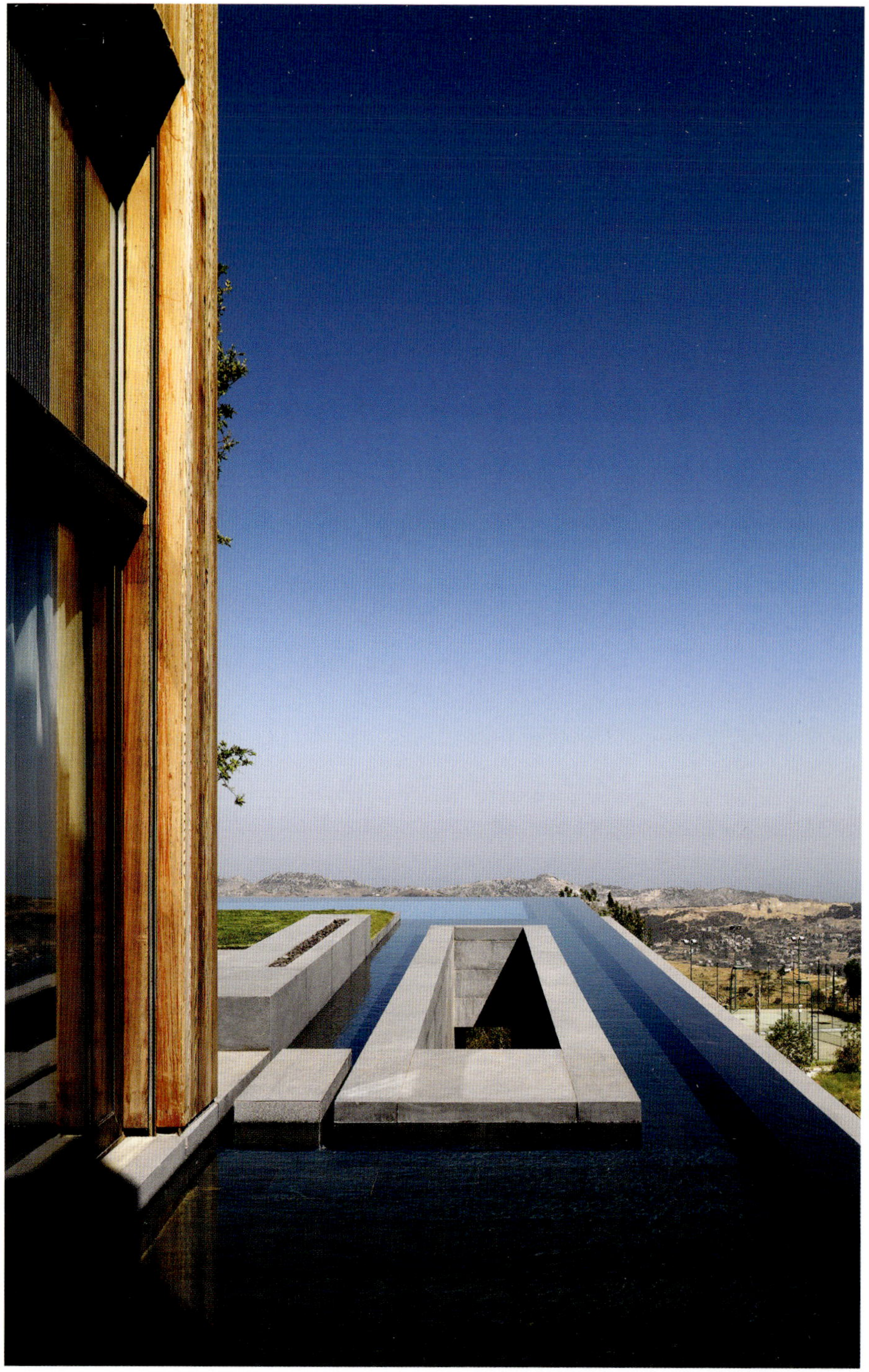

Salame Residence

Located on a steep, remote site near Beirut, this garden space has been transformed into a peaceful sanctuary, offering a retreat from the chaos of city life. Capturing the beauty of the mountain ranges and providing ample space for contemplation, the space also provides room for outdoor entertainment or simply the intimate interactions of friends and family.

The main challenge faced in this landscape intervention was providing safe, usable spaces on a very steep slope. With two simple gestures, the functional, beautiful landscape desired by the clients was achieved. To the front of the home, the granite base of the house was extended, providing the required outdoor space. At the back, a garden was carved into the landscape.

An extensive, multi-purpose water element delineates the garden space to the front of the home, providing a safe boundary that embraces the usable areas of the garden. In addition, the water feature is a functional swimming pool, a place for lounging, playing and exercise. Finally, the water frames and highlights the extensive panoramic views. The shifting lights are reflected upon the water, creating a dynamic element to the landscape juxtaposed by the rigid stone of the pool surrounds.

At the rear of the home, the sunken garden provides a safe, informal, green and organic space carved from the hilltop. This more relaxed, natural space contrasts with the formal expression at the front of the house and provides a play space for children.

Framing stunning panoramic views from every angle and meeting every challenge posed by a difficult site, this is an ideal response to brief. The contrasting spaces, natural and formal, provide a progression of function in which the family can choose to interact, find solitude, play or relax. The recurring grey granite is a strong thematic element, both durable and handsome, that frames the garden and complements the home, completing the space.

Capturing the beauty of the mountain ranges and providing ample space for contemplation, the space also provides room for outdoor entertainment or simply the intimate interactions of friends and family.

Mediterranean Terrace

garden.

About

After years working as a plant buyer for London Garden Centres, Vicky Harris went on to study Garden Design at Capel Manor College, where she graduated with the accolade of 'Best Student' in 2011. Since then she has spent her time as a designer, transforming private gardens into tranquil, yet functional, outdoor spaces.

In 2012 Vicky was given the opportunity by Veolia Water to design an Artisan Garden at the Chelsea Flower Show entitled 'Naturally Dry', for which she received a silver medal. The garden is currently being relocated to Capel Manor College to be enjoyed by students and garden visitors.

Vicky Harris Garden Design
UNITED KINGDOM
T: +44 7 779 252 628
www.vickyharrisgardendesign.co.uk

The unusual triangular shaped site was difficult to disguise, but a layered design mixed with a considered use of balanced hardscaping softens and distracts from the yards' restrictions.

Mediterranean Terrace Garden

The Mediterranean Terrace Garden has an inviting, eclectic charm. The low maintenance plant scheme is interspersed with the client's own plant choices, allowing a greater level of interaction with the garden. The balanced design is traditionally styled, yet the unusual array of plants gives it a diverse and unstructured aspect that works to warm the overall atmosphere.

Traditional Mediterranean products run throughout the garden, providing a base structure for the loose planting scheme to add colour and depth. Terracotta tiles form a hardscaped courtyard, while black tiles are used to define and highlight the space while distracting from the unusual angular form of the garden.

The central pond makes for a beautiful feature. The raised bed and pond walls are rendered and painted white, reflecting light and giving the space a subtle, glimmering pull. The lower walls are topped with a terracotta tile to form additional seating. A Grecian urn, tipped haphazardly on its side, forms the main focus of the garden, with water flowing gently over its lip and into the pond, providing the soothing noise of flowing water and a dynamic visual feature. This is a place for contemplation, where one can watch fish flit around or enjoy the tranquil sound of running water.

The nearby large pergola provides a place where hanging baskets can be suspended, while also contributing shade from the occasional inclement weather and bright summer sun.

An array of hardy Mediterranean plants dominate the garden. The low maintenance greenery is subdued in colour, yet provides an attractive range of textures. Meanwhile, a selection of annual plants break up the scheme with more vibrant hues and depth. Many of the plants are aromatic, including the *lavandula* the *rosmarinus* and the *thyme*, to add an extra layer of enjoyment to the garden.

Photography by: Vicky Harris

The original low maintenance planting scheme implemented by Vicky Harris has been complemented by the addition of the client's own selection of plants.

Jonata

vineyard.

About

William Joyce is the owner and principal designer at William Joyce Design. He began his career in the field with his hands in the earth, building with local stone in New England. Between acquiring his Bachelors and Masters degrees, he spent time working with various trades in the landscape industry, gleaning a true appreciation and passion for the art of Landscape Architecture.

William Joyce Design is a firm, dedicated to creating imaginative, functional and attractive landscapes that elicit a lasting response and are intrinsic to the locality and site. The firm seeks uncontrived, natural solutions designed to generate discovery, splendour and balance.

William Joyce Design
Landscape Architecture and Planning
San Diego, California 92103, United States of America
T: +1 805 705 3564
www.williamjoycedesign.com

The plantscape evolves slowly from the home, which sits atop a knoll in the rolling topography, and connects the modern structure with the landscape.

The Jonata Vineyard Entertainment Home

This picturesque site in Santa Ynez offers a perfect, quintessentially Californian palette of mellow gold and warm green. Cabernet vines, native oaks, grassland, a natural reservoir and local wildlife, all adapted to blistering summers and freezing winters, frame a working farm and a unique, newly built home at the heart of this distinctive retreat.

Encompassing 2.5 acres, this project sought to transform a barren, empty dirt lot surrounding the custom built entertainment home into a beautiful landscaped outdoor space that would reflect the quality and sophistication of the handcrafted boutique wines against the sweeping backdrop of the California vineyard.

William Joyce, the landscape architect has captured the spirit and essence of the spatial connection between the vineyard, the home, and the surrounding natural environment. The landscape design integrates the juxtaposing energies of modern lifestyle, contemporary lines, flashy cars, business suits and fine wines with the rustic warmth of oak woodlands and chaparral, natural wetlands and native fauna.

The plantscape evolves slowly from the home, which sits atop a knoll in the rolling topography, and connects the modern structure with the landscape. Native plants were used preferentially, and non-native plants were only implemented if they were drought tolerant and hardy to the severe environment. Large swathes of grass hold the texture of the garden, keeping it soft. Flowers provide a subtle dash of colour, and bold Agave and succulents round out the textural composition. The native Oaks were important to retain a sense of history and ground the design in locality, and the addition of olives provides the garden with function, as they produce olive oil on site.

By transforming the previously empty dirt lot into a planted, practical space filled with natives, the landscape has been regenerated to the benefit of human visitors to the site, but also to the benefit of the environment.

The Santa Ynez residential vineyard project demonstrates that dedicated landscape and architectural design concepts can be applied to provide functional and attractive designs that enhance the site. This beautiful landscape will endure, balancing a unique and competing blend of practical and aesthetic elements.

Photography by: William Carson Joyce & Jezaira Knight
Landscape Contractor: Down To Earth Landscapes Inc.
General Contractor: David Chavez Construction
Mason: Sean Wooley

This beautiful landscape inspires, entertains and will endure, balancing a unique and competing blend of practical and aesthetic elements.

COS Design – Caulfield North
Photography by: Urban Angles